Pout
of Tangerine Tango

poems by

Victoria Garton

Finishing Line Press
Georgetown, Kentucky

Pout
of Tangerine Tango

Copyright © 2022 by Victoria Garton
ISBN 978-1-64662-919-0 First Edition
All rights reserved under International and Pan-American Copyright Conventions. No part of this book may be reproduced in any manner whatsoever without written permission from the publisher, except in the case of brief quotations embodied in critical articles and reviews.

ACKNOWLEDGMENTS

Grateful acknowledgment is made to the editors of the following publications where these poems—some of which have been revised—first appeared:

anykey ezine: "Serious Hungarians, Happy Americans"
Dial 174: "In Hungary, Troubled Sleep"
Dream Fantasy International: "Wheat, Hungarian Countryside"
Mid-America Poetry Review: "At the Lipizzaner Stable"
POEM: "A Crock of Szmolec" and "Riding Moxie"
The Same: "Bees and Beekeepers" and "What We Encounter, What We Retain"

This collection of poems is dedicated to the generous Fulbright-Hays Seminars Abroad Program that allowed me to spend six weeks in Eastern Europe in the summer of 1998 with a group of American teachers. Their actual names are used in poems only if they have granted permission. I appreciated the opportunity to study the educational systems, lifestyles, and changes that had taken place in Hungary and Poland following the fall of the U.S.S.R. While my focus was on curriculum development, I kept a journal from which these poems grew. These poems are for Huba, Annamaria, Andrez, Ola, and Dorota, our gracious hosts.

Publisher: Leah Huete de Maines
Editor: Christen Kincaid
Cover Art: Victoria Garton
Author Photo: Anne Pool
Cover Design: Elizabeth Maines McCleavy

Order online: www.finishinglinepress.com
also available on amazon.com

Author inquiries and mail orders:
Finishing Line Press
PO Box 1626
Georgetown, Kentucky 40324
USA

Table of Contents

Sunflowers and Lipizzaners

    Taking Measure 1
    Central Hotel, Budapest 2
    After Hungarian, English is Spun Sugar 3
    American Teachers Going to Class 4
    Serious Hungarians, Happy Americans 5
    Robbery on the Way to the Opera—Bela's Story 6
    In Hungary, Troubled Sleep 7
    Midnight Fears 8
    Outside Sopron, Hungary 9
    The Cold War 10
    Bees and Beekeepers 11
    Wheat, Hungarian Countryside 12
    Marzipan Images 13
    At the Lipizzaner Stables 14
    Riding Moxie 15
    Sunflowers and Lipizzaners 16
    A Night of Seduction 17

Into the Salt Mines

    Night Train into Poland 21
    Women on an Early Morning Train 22
    Field Trip to View Peasants 23
    Late Night Krakow 24
    A Crock of Szmolec 25
    Auschwitz Gets Personal 26
    After the Dunajec River 27
    In the Tatra Mountains 28
    Sharing a Log 29
    Going Underground 30
    In Every Group Is a Perpetual-Motion Mouth 31
    What We Encounter and Retain 32
    Pout of Tangerine Tango 33

Sunflowers and Lipizzaners

Taking Measure

Hot summer of 1998 in the Midwest
I pack for Eastern Europe's chilly nights.
Taking measure, I weigh the bag, see myself
dragging it from train to hotel room, remove
a shirt, forgetting the monotony of uniforms.
I'll wear these clothes for six weeks
in the company of sixteen over-packed teachers.

I'm packing too for hills and valleys
of an introvert's terrain. Taking measure,
I weigh elation against the tires-on-pavement
monotony of voices I can't hush, a fading
smile, a lagging spirit, inclines of the heart.

On the bus from the airport, Budapest
surprises with crumbling facades,
entices like faded femme fatale. Samuel,
professor/economist, lectures on western capital.
I try to not take measure as pensioners lift lids
of garbage cans and offer passers-by a bureau,
a picture frame, a chair. Ingénue entrepreneurs,
their shoulders slump. No one stops to buy.

Stepping from the bus, I find my light bag
heavy with rulers and gauges and all the excess
I thought I'd left behind in America.

Central Hotel, Budapest
June 29, 1998

We pass the rumor, famous Communists
sat in the tapestry chairs across the hall,
until everything changed eight years ago.
I sit in a room of dark cherry wood
feeling rich on burgundy cushions
and luxuriate in space unaffordable
in Western Europe or America.
The school shirt I washed in the tub
hangs from the balcony waving
its red, white, and blue. Our mascot,
little blue Patriot, looks jauntily out
on the passing Hungarians. I drag
a massive chair to the balcony,
read Attila Jozsef's grim poetry,
and dry my hair.
In an enclave of embassies,
my white crew socks over the rail
offer limp flags of peace.
No smiles from passers-by or
complaints to management.
Peace comes to me. It is as if
Attila Jozsef, poet on the periphery,
has seriously infected the natives.
Nothing dampens my permanent-press grin.

After Hungarian, English is Spun Sugar

Would songs of angels crystallize
any sweeter than my native tongue?
After Hungarian, English is spun sugar.
Here no words ring familiar. How
do I complement myself or find
my own voice under the roar of traffic
in noisy Budapest? Ivy ripples
over a wall, whispers intimacies
my ringing ears can't hear.
Wind advances on sirens, takes
my attention everywhere but to
the silence where poems wait.
I seek my native language among words
I can't get off my tongue. Long
for English to brush my ears
like angel's wings, angel's hair.

American Teachers Going to Class

Each morning we duck into the tiny shop,
and pass the vats of ice cream, the cooler
of drinks. At the counter I place our order,
"*Kerem ketto espresso.*" The Hungarian
woman asks what we've come to know
is "Do you want cream?" Bill does.
I don't. We take turns handing her the
gold coin with silver rim. The *kave* comes
in tiny cups of white. Black and strong,
the three sips bring us awake to sleepy
Budapest. We'll open a Starbucks here,
bring beans we like from the states.
Working men in coveralls sit on stools
drinking beer from tall brown bottles.
They stare openly at us as does a small
woman with large goiter. Wearing white,
she comes each day to pace like a bride.
She searches each passing face and if
she ever finds a groom, a table waits
for them in the Starbucks of Budapest
Bill and I in dreams have already opened.

Serious Hungarians, Happy Americans

> *"A pessimist is an informed optimist. An optimist is a blind pessimist."*
> Hungarian Philosophy

All morning the rain has fallen on Hero Square
where revolutionaries fell in '56.
The faces of Hungarians are serious,
not full of joy for reclaimed independence.
Eight years beyond the end of Soviet domination
no one dances in the streets.
Freedom has come with a price.

Monkeys in the Budapest zoo sit in iron cages.
All day they preen and scratch under the public eye
while the zoo director's plans go unfunded
and no rich capitalist steps forth as *Donor* or *Patron*.
Hungarians working several jobs do not join
Friends of the Zoo
or volunteer for civic good as reluctantly they did
under the old regime.
The monkeys sit mirroring serious faces of the
staring public.

I walk the streets of Budapest with Scott,
the happiest American in our group. Hungarians
look and look again at his wonder-boy smile,
his appetite for paprika chicken, stuffed cabbage,
and Gundel's chocolate pancakes.
We drink the wines, Eger Bulls Blood and Golden Tokaj.
We pull out credit cards for Zsolnay porcelain
and tee-shirts celebrating the death of Lenin.

Happy capitalists, our enthusiasm is unrelenting.
Our serious hosts stare back as if deprived
of the secure womb of socialism.
They are not yet attuned to the iron cage
of happy, consuming Americans.

Robbery on the Way to the Opera—Bela's Story

What we expected was a dream vacation
with a native guide.
I dress for the opera in my slinky gown,
clutch bag, and naiveté.
We were taken on that first subway ride,
then freed to find our way in a strange city.
One look they know no money belt under
my gown, no passport lanyard between breasts.
Insulated by ignorance of language,
some of us assumed forty years
of communism had erased capitalist greed.
They want my passport, my picture so like
my Hungarian grandmother. Her
close-set eyes gaze from Ellis Island
to this black market where her look sells.
We watched the pick-pockets crowd in,
form a box, block the door. We covered
our pockets, clutched bags, shoved through.
The sting happens fast and they disappear.
We grouped to check valuables. We were
like children robbed of lunch money.

Now on the road at Danube Bend,
unwelcome hands jolt dreams.
At 4:45 a.m. light creeps over the geraniums
in the window box. Sleep has been fitful
at best. Bela gazes out the window,
her face stiff as passport picture.
Honey bees rise up from the hedge. Mist
steals the view of the blue, blue Danube.

In Hungary, Troubled Sleep

Demons and angels wrestle me down.
Like Jacob I sleep on pillow of stone.
Church bells clamor, jar me awake.
Cymbals slice minutes from startled life.

Chestnuts shade a bust of Liszt;
near alyssum I hum a song of home.
Petunias in beds open for natives
who stretch and shuffle off to mass.

Midnight Fears

Your darting eyes attack.
Your trained hand proves too quick.
Against you I strap on money belt,
lock my jewels in hotel safe.

I'm in your face flashing my camera.
I capture you in rags of my midnight fears
and match you sneer for sneer when later
we meet on the steps of St. Matthias.

Someday like a hunter out-staring
a trophy's glass eyes, I'll study your
preyed-upon look that called forth
my fears and left me guilt rich.

Outside Sopron, Hungary

Sapphire blooms,
sprawl of vines,
swollen melons
on hardened ground
roll like heads.

So many died
in WWII.
Hungarian Jews
off to death camps
in the war's
last days.

I'd like to think
I'd never be hard
as this ground.
I'd like to think
I'd never look away.

But, we are headed south
where Bosnia's soil
is soft with blood,
and back home my
pioneer family flourished
on stolen hunting ground.

The Cold War

The Cold War sizzled when Soviet tanks
rolled over Hungarians in Hero's Square.
Nine that year, I drank in peace
from a small carton of milk and read
"My Weekly Reader."
No blood in black and white photographs
but we children of WWII dads saw
freedom as cockroach under Soviet shoe.

The sirens wailed. In line we descended
gray stairs to the boiler room.
Yellow and black signs. Civil Defense.
The furnace roared. In the cafeteria,
water for macaroni boiled.
Bombs mushroomed in our heads.
Fear tasted like canned peas
simmering for lunch.

Those giants Lenin, Engels, and Marx
rose to topple us. Dominoes, we stood to fall.
A girl in Civics class, I bent over books
shaping enemies huge as their statues.
At Freedom Forum and Girls' State,
I marched with Cold War warriors
against such towering monuments.
In 1998 at Szoborpark near Budapest

the giants stood. We tossed Molotov cocktails
of vodka and juice down our own throats.
We sang along with socialist songs,
danced in monumental shadows as night came.
Later, huge tyrant faces and mushroom bombs
invaded sleep. Chased down gray steps,
peace crumbled like pie crust. I awoke
choking on over-cooked peas.

Beekeepers and Lost Bees

Thursday, It Must be Lake Balaton

Our schedule is the queen bee
directing all activity.
We stand behind glass observing
the giant hive at IBM Székesfehérvár.
Workers dressed like beekeepers
make hard drives in clean rooms.
Every four hours they rest for 20 minutes.

We buzz around
yet another huge buffet.
"Hungarians," says Samuel,
"feed guests to keep them happy."
We swarm stones of yet another town.
Think like thoughts as our guide drones.

I step into a shop looking for a bag.
Find I've gone off like a bee enticed
by clover. Lose the group, the bus,
the undisputable schedule, and find myself
happily in a bar where an Irishman
like ancestor from County Down
says, "Come back for a drink at 6:00,
I'll be off work."

Searching for Americans I find Donald
who likes to say, "If I tell you,
I'll have to kill you." He thinks bravado
and my phrase book will get us back
to Budapest. I disagree. The last man
I'd get lost with flits beside me.
Last bees to leave the hive, we fly
over cobblestones flagging our bus.

It is Thursday, we must be in Lake Balaton.

Wheat, Hungarian Countryside

Rain and wind swirl
long fields of wheat.
Stems tilt. Heavy heads
lower their canopy.
Half a world away
Kansas wheat flexes
against the wind's hand.
As I enter the bus
a hand brushes my arm.
A face, my husband's
advances on waving wheat.
Now nice a night of love
would be.
How nice to feel
my husband's hand
brush down my arm like wind
against the ripe and bending
heads of grain.

Marzipan Images

In the Marzipan Museum
a life-sized Michael Jackson
stands true to his image
three surgeries ago.
Behind dark shades, his face
of egg white, ground almond,
and sugar beseeches me
to watch him spin the moon.
In his unmoved audience,
stand usurped Kings of Hungary.
I've chosen altars of marzipan
while Catholics go to mass
and others in our group
turn pasty faces to the sun
or go around Szentendre
in pairs and sets. I go alone
to Margit Kovacs' figurines.
Porcelain grown mysterious
in the artist's hands.
A whimsical girl tends geese.
A woman with slight smile
kneads bread.
Inspired I open my notebook,
but three of our number advance
while moonwalking away.

At the Lipizzaner Stable

Rich dark leather polished, shined, and
hung on display can't forget what was bridled.
Woven thin strips still hold the shape
of prominent nose bones, the smell
of lathered horses. I breathe in the tack,
the golden trophies, the quick-shivering
bodies made to be mounted.

A world away my horse Suzy neighs.

A curious man moves into my space,
reads the engravings and fingers
the leather. He shifts and leans forward
sniffing deeply as if taking in my smell.
I move away quickly, for I am Eve
in the garden suddenly exposed and
aware of no leaf to hide human need.

Riding Moxie

Szalajka Valley, Hungary

Out the bus window,
brown colts and gray mares run
as if lightning still crackled.
Under umbrellas, we walk to where
the *csikós* wears loose blue *gatya*
over knee-high boots.
Silver buttons on his black vest
brighten an overcast day.
His long whip circles overhead
cutting medallions out of gray sky
that seem to drop
into the up-turned brim of his hat.

His horse, Moxie, sits up on haunches,
folds front legs dog-like, sets one hoof
on the cowboy's shoulder, a young wife
in sepia print behind a husband,
one hand comfortably on a shoulder.
Then Moxie is up shaking off submission
as the day brightens shaking off clouds.
Stepping forward, I shake off group fears
to rise up into the saddle and move
to an ancient rhythm.

Moxie and I are sunlight
breaking over the herd, as the herd
with whom I've traveled recedes.
We cut a magic circle and step through.
Later, I ride shotgun on the buckboard
back to the village.
A light rain sprinkles my head,
baptismal water on a redeemed brow.

Sunflowers and Lipizzaners

Traveling Hungarian countryside
tire-tread monotony of late afternoon

sunflowers and lipizzaners look away,
so we turn to see what we missed.

Dark colts and light mares lift on hind legs.
The flowers tune faces to the golden sun.

All synchronize to Bartok's shocking strains.
As horse hooves strike flames, the fields ignite.

A Night of Seduction

On this last night in Budapest,
I whisper the name with an "sh"
hushing all pesky inhibitions,
and accept apricot brandy from the hand
of a Hungarian splendid in navy.
Bridge girders pass overhead
as the Danube drinks the sun
and turns golden.

Between two men whose inflections
argue for something beyond
what is expected and rational,
I nod and smile
at myself
in the middle of life,
in love with a country
I am leaving.

I sip red wine of Sopron,
dream the prized Holy Crown
in the National Museum, while
the men argue. A thumb points east.
fingers cup to the chest what is precious.
Arms cross against a chopping hand
while I lean into the cologne,
the quick masculine breath, look out
to the dusky city sparkling her lights,
tracing bridges, streets, and spires.

If either man pauses to gather
a rose from the table,
I am lost.
But their talk shifts to work,
that brighter mistress,
and something beyond lilting voices

dies as the boat bumps the dock.
Good-byes are as light as a brushed cheek.

I pluck the last rose
and with fellow travelers walk the city
to the high Citadel, where
a lone guitar player plucks strings.

The magnificent moon has his heart
and wants mine. Long ago
a rash boy proclaimed,
"You're in love with love."

I forgive his stabbing rejection,
his steely truth, and toss the rose
to the darkness, accepting
that most focused of lovers, the moon.

Into the Salt Mines

Night Train into Poland

To the sound of steel wheels on rails
we sleep in stacked bunks
fretful of boughs about to break,
lullaby of falling babies.
A chill from open window crawls necks.

Banging at our door brings
language of nightmare. We dig
for passports, put forth documents,
try to squint night faces into
some semblance of photographs.

Our train from Hungary
crosses borders. New uniforms appear.
Sleep is what we imagine
until again angry voices startle
and light accosts eyes.

Gold stars on red epaulets.
We stand by bunks.
Who rehung the iron curtain?
By Poland, sleep-walkers
pull documents.

We dream cattle cars.
Only the thick *z*'s and *k*'s
from mouths of hosts
will save us from sleep's
dangerous terrain.

Women on an Early Morning Train

Three women from America sit
in a sleeper car on a train heading for Krakow.
Midwestern women, they nod
at quilts of contour farming,
lush green potato plants, cabbages in gardens,
and black-eyed Susans bordering the tracks.
Bunks folded, comforters rolled into bolsters,
toothbrushes and clothes packed; they sit
and do not comment on the old woman riding
a rusted bike to early morning chores.

Three men from America stand in the aisle.
In their sleeper car, bunks are a snarl of covers.
Each man strokes an unshaved chin,
talks loudly over the grinding wheels.
Occasionally, the men glance to where
the women sit serene with welcoming laps
like mothers once did at sunrise. The women
do not turn from graffiti-covered walls,
from coal in open railroad cars passing close,
from Polish names on peeling facades.

These women sit in their ordered world
as if they've had enough of eager, unkempt men
at day-break. They lean a little to the window
with its passing fence heavy with roses.
Finally, when one of the men leans in
about to speak, rollers slide in the track
shutting the door. The bolt clicks, resolute
as a mother's tongue sending him off
to his morning chores.

Field Trip to View Peasants

Our professors prepared us by always using *lazy*
before *peasants*. Through the bus window
we see close rows of crosses someone planted
and potato plants waving white blooms
and heavy-headed grain tied into shocks.
Someone erected life-sized shrines to Virgin Mary
and laid bedding over second-story windows
and planted purple and white petunias.
Pitchforks of hay land on flat wagons.
On spiked poles the hay rounds neatly like
ice cream on cones. We look under each, but
no one lies sleeping. Finally on a road winding
from patchwork fields, we see Polish peasants.
Old men lean on spades and drive old tractors.
Old women with kerchief-tied cabbage heads
chop and chop with short-handled hoes
that pull them into greenery. In air-conditioned buses
we watch this scene melt into hot mid-day sun.

We must ask our professors why lazy peasants
even bother to grow turnips, rutabaga, and chard.

Late Night Krakow

Navy clouds have bruised the sky
bringing night and stalled time.
Bill sits with me talking trash
as if to lure shielding darkness.
It finally comes with stars like ellipses.
Bill, ignoring the peace of omitted words,
natters on about loved ones in America.
Balm for his absence, he concludes,
"At this moment they see the same stars."

I look at my watch,
proclaim it 3:00 p.m. and sunny
in the Midwest where I live.
I leave him sitting on the cold bench,
walk half a block, stop and turn,
"You coming?"

A Crock of Szmolec

In Krakow I can't savor the veal
at Chlopskie Jadlo
for savoring my anger.
I stare at the crock of *Szmolec*,
rendered pork fat, onion, garlic,
black pepper, and salt,
no one chooses to spread
on slabs of white bread.
I see it heaped on the head
of the man to my left.

I chew and chew the dry bread
as if chewing the rude rebuff
passed like rendered fat
on the haughty arrogance
of the man to my left.
Between us an unclaimed knife.
With it I slice
Szmolec from the heaping crock,
lather the cheek to my left.

In my hardened heart, the knife tip
goes on point, dances
my anger in blood, replaces
that sneer with bright graffiti.
In truth, only my face grows red.
By-passing the pink-hued *Szmolec*,
I grow fat on anger while
the man on my left
savors his veal.

Auschwitz Gets Personal

Brick buildings stand sturdy, but the fence
of tall concrete poles demands attention.
Tops bend sideways into listening ears.
Stubby insulators like amputated limbs
support rows of electrified barbed wire.
Few escaped or believed the lie
Arbeit Macht Frei—Work Makes You Free—
in huge letters over the entry gate.
Still, symmetry of wrought iron
pleases a need for order. One can enter
without horror and walk to the concrete building.
Smelling from the long trip, given a bar of soap,
one enters willingly. How hard to die on concrete,
stomach griped in pain, lungs filling with gas.
Cyclon B containers behind glass testify, as do
tiny clothes taken from babies. In the room
of shoes an open-backed sandal
in red, white, and blue stays fashionable.
Someone ripped its sole searching for jewels.
That shoe was worn by a young woman
with a slight swish to the hips. Lightly she stepped
on Warsaw's streets in the spring. Luxurious
hair swung from side to side. Shaved,
it dropped and joined these piles of hair,
or went to Germany to stuff a mattress. Maybe
a tired soldier slept on her hair with his wife.
Maybe they conceived a child and tried to forget.
It's hard to forget that shoe or decals on suitcases
in the room of old baggage still waiting to be claimed.

After the Dunajec River

The trip is available to all brave enough to leave home.

In Zakopane the heart is a tiny steel ball
rolling from the Pieniny Mountains,
to a dark wooden church,
to the sharp face of Giewont.
Mine lodges for a moment
in a makeshift stall
where I finger course wool
and buy a sweater against the chill
caught after rain peppered my back
on the Dunajec River.

Sometimes when we travel,
weather pierces our thoughts,
but first the sky clots
and clouds promise a deluge.
Before the flat boats fill with water
comes that moment for which we
packed umbrellas, raincoats, and courage.
Because of this moment
some never leave home,
and some never return
to where the heart lost its way
and followed the cow wandering
the lawn of Helios Hotel, chewing
heads of sweet clover.

In the Tatra Mountains

Sketched in charcoal
against an azure sky,
the Tatras, uneroded and young,
wait in pristine air
to offer cotton-candy clouds
to those who hike.

According to legend
sleeping knights awaken
to bring freedom.
With the Iron Curtain
smashed, they seem to move
with the wind toward
Slovakia.

Meanwhile, young men bring
steaming vodka with green tea,
kraut and beef soup,
bacon and onions skewered,
deep-fried potatoes,
cheese from a goat, and walnuts
in gelatin.

They bang a shield
over a vent, worry the peace
of chatting middle-aged ladies,
snicker and run for the kitchen.
Their suspenders embroidered
with red and black flowers
wait to be snapped.

When sleeping knights awakened
in the Tatras, they fathered
these laughing young men
who extend a paddle with a sweet
to any moneyed tourist
looking peeved.

Sharing a Log

> *Even when language, coin, and custom seem strange, we enter familiar shadows.*

Like a wooly worm, the funicular crawls
up the ridge west of Zakopane.
I shed my wooly sweater
as the sun cures hay on poles.

Parents extend strange coins
so children can sit in awe
on the ponies stepping a sure circle.
Tinkling bells can't dim the shrill boys
descending on sluice rides.

Anne, Vera, and I escape to a thicket of spruce,
a place of cool shadows
from which the view unfolds.
Farms define themselves
by tree-line and shades of green.
Cottages sprout like mushrooms after rain.

We sit in silence asking nothing
of the moment. No need
to hear our own voices or claim this place
by bragging up its beauty.

We have traveled far to get
to this Sunday afternoon,
this shared log, these familiar shadows.

Going Underground

Men no longer sweat and toil in
the Wieliczka Salt Mines.
Saints abide, along with the savior
carved in hard gray salt.
Salty tears run at news from home.

My niece, age 29, has cervical cancer.
I feed cards into a phone,
listen for hope in familiar voices.
Face a wall in a coffee shop,
nurse a cappuccino, cry alone.

Happiness for me lives above ground,
but open windows slam. I plummet
down an elevator shaft. In salty earth
I've known a friend's death,
a son's broken neck, my own tumors.

Late night off Krakow square,
my niece and I discuss surgery,
children who won't be born, chances
of a long life defined by percent.
Oddly, her odds sound good.

Bill like a saint blessing the pay phone
hands out *Zlotych* to beggars and
waits to walk me safely home,
though neither of us know the way
and *home* is an ocean away.

In Every Group Is a Perpetual-motion Mouth.

His narrates the videos
he makes of every town,
every cathedral, every old woman
on rusted bike, every unguarded yawn.
An extrovert with one issue, his voice,
a monotone, worms it into lectures
on Poland's history, economics,
and future. Back in America,
he has a wonderful life,
a wife at home tending many children.
He loves traveling without them,
so he can build them into characters
of a story none of us would read
given a choice.

She likes to talk about the obvious.
She talks about everything she sees.
She grows orgasmic at every stork's
nest on a chimney. She cries
with unbridled passion at bridges,
haystacks, and great art.
Directs operas as the bus rolls,
sings off-key. Has been a professor
all her pedantic life.
In the final week she gets the trots,
stops the bus at every station
from Gdansk to Warsaw.
"Leave her behind," is the vote,
save one.

He thinks we've heard too much
of ethnic cleansing,
can't believe we've forgotten
Auschwitz so fast, suspects
we're all abortionists at heart,
will pray for whomever
said, "Kill the prattling extroverts."

What We Encounter, What We Retain

Plunk go the apples on the roof
as our bus finds ever narrower lanes.
Women pull and tie bunches of wheat,
which men feed to a contraption
of boards and frames. My grandfather
talked of thrashing grain.

Plunk go the strings of bass punctuating
a melody squeezed from accordion
to clarinet to violin. Plunk go the boots
of women dancing on the porch, singing
with fists defiant on waists, heads
at a cocky tilt luring men to pleasure.

Plunk go our feet in a Polish folk dance
our host leads in the summer night.
Under a windmill slicing slivers of moon,
he recites poems. Plunk go the spoons
against china as we circle the ham,
the potatoes, the pastries.

Plunk go the strings as harpist in pearls,
diamonds, and chiffon teases melodies.
Between 16th century ballads, our host tells
story on story of the besieged, the suffering,
the forgotten, the redeemed.

Plunk goes my heart as walking in his
basement I encounter wooden folk figures
and jubilant sneers on guards raising clubs
over a tiny man in white and blue stripes
at the mouth of an oven.

Plunk go the lips of our host on my cheek
saying farewell and startling with affection.

Pout of Tangerine Tango

Wheels of our bags complained
over cobblestones as if they'd caught
the ache of muscles cramped
from a night on the train.
A festoon of pennants
greeted us from the ceiling of the bus
we rode through Krakow.
The Madonna twirled against pink
too garish for a sunrise. Her lips
in a pout of Tangerine Tango, the very shade
I wore in junior high.

Later, I met Madonna of alabaster lips
looking down from golden niche
in the Carmelita Church. Later still,
at Częstochowa, the Black Madonna's dark lips
held firm as supplicants came for miracles.
Looking for Madonna of the good heart,
I chewed my lips at Auschwitz, tasted salt
after Wieliczka, and ended up buying
a brighter lipstick to honor the blood
under the streets of Warsaw.

Once home I dreamed the bell
off Krakow's Square, the one hanging
darkly against stucco, the one whose chime
brought prayers to speed up painful death.
My mother tossed her tube of Shocking Pink
into a drawer, would not dress up for cancer.
Lips set firm, she prayed to Dr. Kavorkian,
"Come quick." I prayed to all the Madonnas
for painless death. She lasted to the New Year,
confetti still fluttering like that pennant
of the Tangerine Madonna.
She died with alabaster lips.
I bought the children of her church
a set of chimes in red, orange, and pink.
They play by color while my mother's spirit
swirls the Tangerine Madonna.

In her extensive travels, **Victoria Garton** journals and then simmers impressions and details into poems. Since she was a teen reading the tattered copy of Robert Frost's "Stopping by the Woods" kept by her bed, poetry has been a way to explore life and the emotions it stirs. In a poetry class with Dave Smith in 1975 she began writing and was soon publishing. Her work has been published in many journals and her first book, *Kisses in the Raw Night*, was published by BkMk Press. She holds an Educational Specialist Degree from University of Missouri and taught English and Literature classes for Crowder College for 15 years following a career in high school teaching. She and her husband raise Angus cattle on a ranch in Nevada, MO, and have two sons and two granddaughters.

www.ingramcontent.com/pod-product-compliance
Lightning Source LLC
LaVergne TN
LVHW041556070426
835507LV00011B/1126